D1128658

A Picture Book of

SWAMP and MARSH ANIMALS

Written by Theresa Grace
Illustrated by Roseanna Pistolesi

Troll Associates

BLACK BEAR

Black bears aren't always black. Some are brown, and others can even be partly white. These quiet, slow animals spend a lot of time looking for food. They will eat just about anything, including berries, fish, small animals, plants, and honey.

Bears have to eat a lot in the summer and fall. Many of them spend the cold winter months sleeping in a safe, warm den in a log or cave. There, the female gives birth to 1 to 4 cubs. These tiny cubs have no fur, and their eyes are closed. But the cubs grow fast. When they grow up, they will weigh between 200 and 500 pounds (90–225 kilograms)! Cubs live with their mother for 1 or 2 years, learning all the things a bear needs to know to survive in the wild.

Library of Congress Cataloging-in-Publication Data

Grace, Theresa.
   A picture book of swamp and marsh animals / by Theresa Grace;
illustrated by Roseanna Pistolesi.
       p.   cm.
   Summary: Spotlights more than a dozen creatures found in swamps
and marshes including the box turtle, manatee, pelican, and
alligator.
   ISBN 0-8167-2434-2 (lib. bdg.)   ISBN 0-8167-2435-0 (pbk.)
   1. Swamp fauna—Juvenile literature.   2. Marsh fauna—Juvenile
literature.   [1. Swamp animals.   2. Marsh animals.]   I. Pistolesi,
Roseanna, ill.   II. Title.
QL113.8.G73   1992
591.52'6325—dc20   91-16034

Printed in the United States of America.
10 9 8 7 6 5 4 3 2 1

ALLIGATOR

Alligators like to live in fresh water. The shape of its head lets an alligator keep its eyes and nose above the water as it swims.

Fish, frogs, birds, snakes, and other animals that live near water are an alligator's favorite food. Alligators are very strong. A large alligator can pull a dog, a pig, or other large animals into the water.

Female alligators lay 20 to 60 eggs in a nest made of wet grass and other plants. Young alligators live with their mother for about a year. Babies are only about 9 inches (23 centimeters) long when they are born, but a full-grown male alligator is 9 to 12 feet (2.7–3.6 meters) long and can weigh over 500 pounds (225 kilograms)!

KING SNAKE

It is not easy to find a king snake. These animals are shy, and like to hide under rocks and logs. They come out at night to hunt for other snakes, which they like to eat. The king snake kills its prey by *constricting*, or wrapping its body so tightly around the animal that its victim cannot breathe. Then the snake swallows the animal whole!

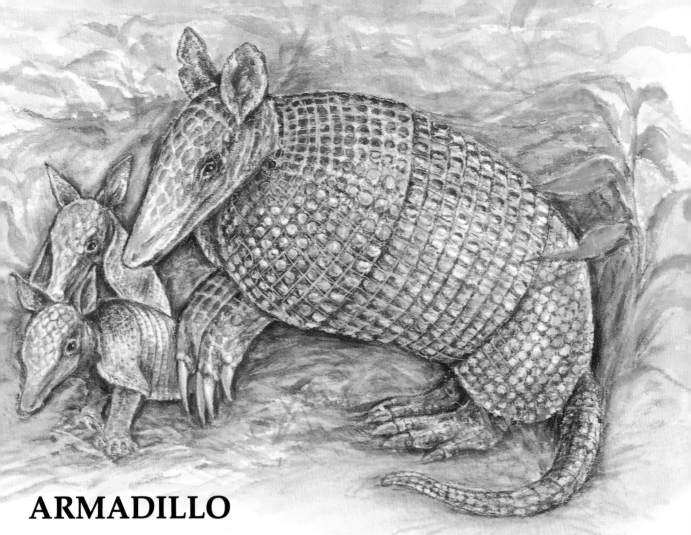

ARMADILLO

These odd-looking animals are covered with bony plates. This shell protects the animal from prickly thorns as it hurries through the thick brush. When too far from its burrow, the armadillo escapes from enemies by digging quickly into the ground with its strong claws.

An armadillo eats many insects that are harmful to crops. It licks up insects with its long, sticky tongue.

When an armadillo is surprised, it does a very odd thing. It jumps straight up in the air!

KITE

This large bird is so at home in the air, it almost never touches the ground. It swoops down to catch frogs, insects, small birds, and snakes, then eats them as it flies! The kite's 3½-foot (1-meter) wingspan lets it soar easily through the sky, while its forked tail helps the bird steer and slow down.

Kites nest high in the trees. They raise one chick at a time. It is hard work. The chick eats almost nonstop, so the parents are very busy catching food for their hungry child.

RIVER OTTER

Few animals are as playful and fun to watch as an otter. From balancing pine cones on its nose to sliding down an icy hill into the water, an otter loves to play.

River otters actually live in swamps, marshes, and small lakes. There is plenty of their favorite foods in these places: fish, frogs, crabs, and other small animals.

An otter's thick fur helps it live in cold, wet places. Its webbed paws help it swim quickly, and special muscles close its nose and ears so the otter can swim underwater.

GREAT BLUE HERON

A heron is one of a group of birds called *wading birds*. The great blue heron is the largest kind of heron in America. This bird likes to wade along the shore on its long, thin legs. Its eyes peer down into the water, looking for fish, frogs, and other small animals to eat. When it spots something tasty, the heron quickly bends its head and catches its prey in its long, thin *bill*, or beak.

Herons nest in groups called *flocks*. A heron gathers sticks together to build its nest in a tree or a bush. Females lay 3 to 6 eggs. The young herons cannot take care of themselves. It is up to their parents to hunt for food and bring it to the chicks.

ROSEATE SPOONBILL

This bird's name tells you what it looks like. *Roseate* (RO-zee-it) means rose-colored. This describes the bird's rosy-pink feathers. And its beak is shaped a lot like a spoon. The spoonbill swings its beak through the water to catch the fish, insects, and small crabs it likes to eat.

Roseate spoonbills live where it is warm. Large groups, called *colonies*, live together. They build their nests out of sticks in small trees and bushes.

FIDDLER CRAB

This animal *burrows*, or digs, a home in the mud in marshes and in wet sand on the beach. It likes to eat water plants.

The fiddler crab got its name because males move their large front claw back and forth. It is the same movement a fiddler uses to play the violin.

BOX TURTLE

Imagine carrying your house on your back! That's what a turtle does. When they are frightened, most turtles can pull their head, legs, and tail into their shell. The shell is very hard and strong. It keeps the turtle safe from danger.

Box turtles like to eat insects and fruit. A female lays 4 or 5 eggs in early summer, and the eggs hatch about 3 months later. Box turtles may live to be 80 years old!

PELICAN

Mr. Pelican, what a big beak you have! The bottom part of a pelican's beak is really a pouch made of skin. A group of pelicans will swim along the water in a line to drive fish into the shallow water. Then each pelican scoops up some fish in its pouch.

Pelicans nest together in large colonies. Some kinds of pelicans build nests in trees. Others nest on the ground. Females lay 2 or 3 eggs. About a month later, tiny chicks are born. They have no feathers at first, but after about 3 months they are able to fly.

MINK

This animal's long, thin body helps it slip between rocks and logs in search of muskrats, mice, snakes, and other animals to eat. Mink also dive into the water to catch fish and frogs. Their thick coat has two layers to protect them in the cold water. The top layer is oily, which keeps water away from the mink's body. The inner layer of fur is soft and thick. This keeps the mink warm.

Despite its small size, a mink can be very fierce. When it is angry, a mink will spit and squeal. It makes a lot of noise for an animal that only weighs about 2 pounds (.9 kilogram)!

MANATEE

These large animals are also called sea cows. They swim slowly through the water, using their flippers and broad, flat tail to move along.

Manatees grow to be about 14 feet (4.3 meters) long, and they weigh about 1,500 pounds (675 kilograms). But the only food they eat is plants. A manatee uses its top lip and strong teeth to pull up weeds and grass from the bottom of rivers and other waterways. It can eat more than 100 pounds (45 kilograms) of plants in one day.

WHITE IBIS

It's easy to spot an ibis (EYE-bis)—just look for its long, curved, red bill. This bird likes to wade along the shore, poking its beak in the mud to find insects, frogs, and crayfish.

After they have eaten, ibises fly back to their nests. Ibises live in huge colonies. Sometimes thousands of birds build nests together in trees or reeds along the shore.

WOOD DUCK

Like other kinds of ducks, male and female wood ducks look very different from each other. Males are very colorful. Females are brown, with yellow and white feathers underneath.

Wood ducks like to live in swamps, ponds, and other wet places. They paddle through shallow water, looking for seeds, acorns, and insects to eat. Unlike most ducks, wood ducks nest in trees. Females lay up to 15 eggs. When the chicks are born, they must jump from the tree to the ground. Then they follow their mother into the water.

CROCODILE

Crocodiles look a lot like alligators. But the shape of their heads can help you tell them apart. An alligator's jaw is rounded, but a crocodile has pointed jaws. And some of a crocodile's bottom teeth stick out when its mouth is closed.

A crocodile makes its home in salty water. Crocodiles can be very mean and fierce. They sometimes attack large animals. But fish, birds, and turtles are what they usually eat.